Isabel George is a writer, journalist and PR, who has worked with animal charities, and particularly the PDSA, for many years. She has previously written for children and has also worked with the Imperial War Museum on various events and exhibitions connected with the Animals at War theme.

Also by Isabel George:

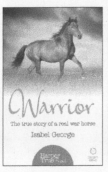
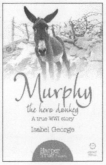
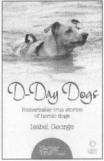

The 9/11 Dogs

The 9119 Door

The 9/11 Dogs

The heroes who searched for survivors at Ground Zero

Isabel George

Harper
True Friend

1 London Bridge Street, London SE1 9GF

HarperTrueFriend
An imprint of HarperCollins*Publishers*

www.harpertrue.com
www.harpercollins.co.uk

First published by HarperTrueFriend 2014

Isabel George asserts the moral right to
be identified as the author of this work

A catalogue record of this book is
available from the British Library

ISBN: 978-0-00-810509-9

'A dog comes into its own when the chances of survival are against it.'

New York firefighter

Foreword

Lower Manhattan, New York, March 2002. I stood on the waterfront just a stone's throw from Ground Zero. Inadequately dressed for the bite of a New York winter, I clenched the short stack of press packs I had been carrying for the past two hours closer to my chest. That morning, the CNN weather reporter announced that this would be the coldest day of the year so far, yet I had still managed to leave my hotel room without gloves and a scarf. I quickly discovered that a bundle of slim paper folders and my thin English wool coat were no match for a minus-twenty wind chill.

Trying hard not to visibly shudder, I looked into the crowd ahead for a distraction. There must have been around 300 people gathered to watch this unique medal ceremony. Television crews and photographers were taking up their positions by the stage, where the soon-to-be-honoured guests included City of New York police and fire officers, alongside search-and-rescue teams and their counterparts from all over the United States. As they mingled with the dark-suited civilians, including representatives from the British Embassy and the Mayor's office, the gold braid on their dress uniforms glistened in the flashes of winter sun. And at their feet, the canine heroes of the hour obediently sat, wondering what all the fuss was about.

German Shepherds, Labradors and spaniels accounted for the majority of the four-legged guests. Some of the dogs were in their dress uniform too, with coats bearing the emblem of the organisation they were representing. For two Golden Labradors – Salty and Roselle – six months earlier the walk into Lower Manhattan would have been a daily part of their routine. These two guide dogs knew this place well, as their masters had worked in the World Trade Center and the dogs had accompanied them into the city every day. If they had any memory of the last time they were in this part of town it would have been a traumatic recollection of leading their owners down over seventy floors of the North Tower and running through a cloud of thick, grey ash surrounded by screaming people fearing for their lives.

That day they were meeting colleagues, police and rescue workers they had not seen since 9/11, and the dogs were enjoying the praise and attention of everyone around them. This was, after all, their day – a presentation ceremony devoted to acknowledging the courage of the dogs who played a vital role during and after the terrorist attack on 11 September 2001. Dedicated search dogs now stood beside devoted guide dogs, and the canines who came to offer comfort and solace to the exhausted and the bereaved. Warm breath rose from the dogs' damp muzzles and drifted into the icy air. Everyone gathered that morning was there to see one thing – the dogs honoured for their loyalty in the face of human tragedy.

As the British High Commissioner took his place on the podium, the handlers checked that the dogs were forming a straight line behind him. With military precision they stood tall. Even Salty and Roselle took the hint that this was a time to sit rather than lie down. A hush fell and all eyes turned to the line of dogs on the stage and the small table where three large bronze medals had been arranged for presentation. In my elevated position at the back of the crowd, I had a full view of the stage. As part of the team involved in putting this presentation together, I knew the stories behind all the dogs and their people. I had worked on the speech that was about to be delivered and knew I would be mouthing every word, but still the enormity of this occasion, which had brought so many people together to honour these incredible dogs, hit hard. Despite the location and the normally bustling time of day, nothing stirred to break the tranquillity of that moment. Cutting clearly through the cold air, the speech was a sombre commemoration of all that was lost that day in 2001, and a celebration of the animal courage and exceptional devotion displayed by the guide dogs who remained devoted to their duty and the search dogs who stepped onto the smouldering pile. Even the dogs listened intently, unaware that they were the centre of everyone's attention.

The 'old man' of the NYPD K-9 unit – a German Shepherd named Appollo – looked to his handler, as if to ask, 'What's going on here?' His big feet restlessly pawed the ground and his huge pink tongue licked around his greying muzzle. He looked nervous on the stage, but for a police search dog with more than eight years' experience, sitting still was not likely to be a favourite pastime. He was not alone. Just along from Appollo sat another German Shepherd, Charlie, who looked more like a golden-coated bear than a regular search dog. He was also trying to encourage his handler to move along and get working. It was taking all the female officer's powers of persuasion to hold her playful canine companion in check, much to the amusement of her colleagues.

Standing still against the wall of cold air, I sensed someone at my side, and as I looked to my right I raised my eyes to meet the gaze of a handsome man wearing a yellow hard hat and a red chequered shirt under a reflective jacket. At his feet a German Shepherd sat looking forward into the crowd, but every now and then he exchanged glances with the man. Maybe he was trying to tell his master that he wanted to join the other dogs sitting on the stage. He certainly looked excited, and his bushy ginger-and-black tail wagged as he sat patiently on the cold ground. The big dog shivered, the cold penetrating his thick, damp coat. I knew how he felt. Then, without a word, the man reached across and gently prised my right hand away from the folders in my frozen grip. Opening my hand, he placed a small thermo heat pad into the palm and closed my fingers around its instant warmth. Then he took my left hand and repeated the process.

'Thank you,' I said.

'That's OK, ma'am,' he replied.

Quickly switching both heat pads and the bundle of papers to one hand, I reached down to pat the dog, a big warm nuzzle meeting my cold fingers. As he pushed his head into my coat I noticed that he, too, was in his working gear. His reflective jacket was spattered with globs of hardened mud and his paws were as dirty as his master's boots.

'Hello, boy. You OK?' I said, sinking my hands into the dog's deep fur until it reached his warm skin. As if to answer me, the dog turned and in an instant licked my face from chin to forehead. Rising to my feet, I said 'thank you' and gave one more pat to the great dog's head. He looked at me and then at his master and seemed pleased that he had made a new friend. I couldn't help wondering if the man and his

5

dog had walked over from Ground Zero to watch the ceremony, and maybe they had. The site was still being cleared and the skills of a CSI dog would be essential now the search was down to detecting traces of the human loss. It seemed appropriate that this team, still in action, would witness medals being bestowed on the four-legged heroes.

Many heroes were made on that day and in the weeks that followed. Not all of them showed human courage. Some of them could only show that they were truly man's best friend. Over 300 search-and-rescue dogs worked 'the pile' at Ground Zero and the crash site at the Pentagon. The New York Police Department's K-9 unit and the city's Fire Department search dogs worked alongside teams from all over the United States. They walked, drove and hitched lifts into Lower Manhattan where, in the chaos, the Federal Emergency Management Agency (FEMA) welcomed the volunteer search-and-rescue teams. Within hours of the North Tower collapsing, the dogs were on duty. Wearing their harnesses, and some in jackets, they padded through the hot ash and weaved among the ruins of twisted metal and broken glass in the hope of finding life. Desperate to recover their colleagues, rescue workers tore into the rubble with their bare hands. Trusting the dogs to locate those buried, they called out for the dogs to help – 'Dog over here! Dog over here!' – and the dogs entered the danger zones. For hours they searched, fighting off exhaustion with sheer determination, and they continued every day long after the hope of finding survivors had passed.

The faithful guide dogs who helped their sightless owners out of the Twin Towers and led them to safety showed unstinting devotion in the face of adversity. Later, the therapy dogs arrived to bring comfort to the bereaved and confused. At every stage of the operation, dogs were there helping humankind in various roles. And invaluably, they provided comfort and reassurance and lifted people's spirits purely by their presence.

The dogs sitting dutifully at the feet of their owners and handlers on the stage were to receive the 'animals' VC' – the equivalent of the British Victoria Cross and the US Medal of Honour – for conspicuous gallantry in the face of conflict. Awarded by the charity PDSA (the People's Dispensary for Sick Animals, founded in London in 1917), the Dickin Medal was instituted in 1943 and was quickly recognised throughout the world as the highest honour for animal bravery in any theatre of war.

From that moment on 14 September when President George W. Bush declared war on terrorism, the dogs' significant role in the aftermath of the 11 September attack gained deserved recognition. Their actions had taken place at the heart of the conflict and the speech at their medal presentation reflected the respect of a grateful nation. The dogs' 'heroic deeds' and their 'steadfast loyalty' during that incredible time prompted a long and strong round of applause. As I glanced around I noticed that there were people wiping tears from their faces. There was open emotion wherever I looked, and the gentle giant beside me with the dog at his heels clapped his hands as he joined in the praise pouring out for the canine teams. The ceremony represented a sentiment long overdue for the handlers – reassurance that their contribution mattered and all their efforts were not in vain.

It is unlikely the dogs were aware of their invaluable contribution to the search that began that warm September morning. They were working and following their canine instinct, applying learnt skills in extraordinary circumstances. Just by being on the scene these dogs influenced human behaviour. Dogs can only be honest. They never make demands or ask the impossible, and they never think anyone is foolish – even when humans think differently. The Ground Zero dogs stepped in as deeply generous, trusted and non-judgemental friends at a time when those qualities were needed more than ever.

Remembering the day when most of the Western world stood still, there remains an inspirational message in the many instances of canine bravery that proved, beyond a shadow of a doubt, that a partnership based on unconditional love can be the most powerful of all.

Guiding to Safety

'Come on, Roselle, let's see if we can reach the subway a little earlier this morning. What do you think, girl?' Michael Hingson knelt down to touch the faithful Golden Labrador at his feet. He stroked her face, his voice soft and reassuring, as he reached over to the kitchen chair for her harness. He smiled, knowing Roselle would be getting excited as the harness meant they were going out together, and that was all that mattered to her. Roselle had been Michael's guide dog for the past two years and she knew his every move.

Setting out early for work was no problem for her, as the journey to Michael's office on the 78th floor of the World Trade Center's North Tower was not just part of her routine; it was the highlight of her day. From the moment she left her family's home in New Jersey she knew that the sidewalks would be infused with new and interesting smells, and on the subway she always met plenty of friendly people wanting to say hello. It's not easy for any dog, not

9

even a guide dog, to be 100 per cent focused on their job, but Roselle never allowed herself to be distracted.

From her first day in training she would have learnt the importance of absolute devotion to her owner. And in all disciplines Roselle was a star pupil. She was a lively and inquisitive puppy who grew into a lively and inquisitive dog, picking up the throb of New York life beneath her paws.

'OK, Roselle. I'm just about ready, so let's see if we can make this early start.' Roselle trotted to Michael's side and the two of them walked out of the house and hailed a taxi to take them to the subway station. Roselle loved riding in the car and immediately lay down happily on the floor. In just a short while they would be heading into the city and starting their working day.

Although Michael could not see the queues of commuters jostling for space on the platform, he could sense an unusual bustle and restlessness around him. Raised voices filled the closed space and mingled with the sea of people waiting for news on the trains going their way. Roselle had seen it all many times before and she knew she must wait for Michael to indicate that they were heading for the information desk. 'Well, I guess that's the end of our plans for an early start, girl. Never mind. We'll get there when we get there. I'd best call David and tell him what's going on.'

The 9/11 Dogs

Michael's colleague David Frank was flying in from California to oversee the team of distributors attending several seminars taking place at the office that day. Both men, who had become great friends while working for the computer software firm, looked forward to this kind of event, as it gave them a chance to meet and catch up on family news and mutual acquaintances. Just as Michael finished making the call to David on his mobile, a train rolled in and Roselle made her presence felt among the people waiting for the carriage door to open. As the happy, swaggering guide dog led her master to a seat, Michael was already thinking over what he still had to do in the office before the first seminar started at 9 a.m.

There was a lift direct from the subway to Michael's offices and the journey seemed even shorter than usual that morning. It was one of those mornings where, once off the train, people seemed to be absorbed into their routes to the nearby offices and apartments. Roselle sensed that Michael wanted to pick up the pace a little, so she responded by breaking out into a slow trot from her steady walk, raising her shiny black nose as she padded along with Michael at her side.

7.40 a.m.: Despite the early hour, it was surprising how many people were already working away on the 78th floor of Tower One that day. Michael could hear plenty of people moving around and guessed that they, too, were caught up in the stir to get a head start on their schedule before the first of the four seminars began. Thankfully he was there in advance of the fifty delegates travelling in specially, and a few of Michael's colleagues were there too, so Roselle received her usual welcome of fuss and attention. Although she was still in harness, and therefore still officially on duty, Michael had no problem releasing her into the hands of his colleagues. They had only been in partnership a short time, but he knew this guide dog could be trusted to mix the business of being Michael's eyes with the pleasure of being everyone's friend. That was what was so special about Roselle: she inspired an unspoken bond of trust that went beyond normal understanding.

Without a word spoken or a physical sign given, Roselle suddenly bowed away from her adoring crowd and took her usual place under Michael's desk. She could always be relied on never to be more than a few inches away from him at any time of the day or night.

8 a.m.: Michael had had time to organise some last-minute tasks before David arrived and they got together to run through the programme for the day. The delegate packs were ready and waiting on the welcome table, the water bottles and coffee were on

order and, at a little after 8.30 a.m., there was only
one thing left to do – compile a check list of attend-
ees and hand it to the World Trade Center security
team at reception.

As the first five delegates made their way across
the Plaza, Michael and David decided there was
just enough time to enjoy another cup of coffee
before the meeting and greeting began. They
smiled as Roselle sighed, stretched her legs and
relaxed her body to fill the space left for her under
the desk. David, who was very fond of Roselle, told
her how lucky he thought she was: 'What a lovely
life you have, girl. No wonder you are so totally
laid-back!' As he spoke David stretched out his
hand to stroke the dog's head. Her eyes closed
under his touch.

8.46 a.m.: Reaching over the printer for stationery,
Michael heard a muffled thud. He didn't think much
of it. It was an unusual noise and one his mind
couldn't place, but that happened all the time.
'Suddenly the building toppled sideways, right under
my feet. The movement shifted me twenty feet
across the room and I heard David call out, "My
God!" Clearly he didn't know what was going on but
I had to ask him: "What happened there?" I was a
blind man asking a sighted man for a view of the
world outside the window on the south side of the
Tower. Talking out loud he said there was nothing

unusual on the skyline. Everything, he said, looked normal.'

As the shifting subsided and levelled out, a loud creaking noise filled the room. Growing up in California, Michael had learnt from an early age that the safest place to stand during an earthquake was in a doorway with the protection of the lintel overhead. There was no better advice to follow right then as the Tower's skeleton heaved and swayed beneath them. The eerie creaking of the metal expansion joints as they stretched like giant springs left everyone suspended in fear.

Michael's immediate concern was for Roselle, and he called to David to check that she was still under the desk. He was reassured that she was fine and in that moment Michael felt his own anxiety fall away. It had become the way of their partnership that Michael would take his lead from Roselle: if she was calm then he could allow himself to be calm too.

Suddenly, from somewhere out of the confusion, a decision was taken by someone to evacuate the entire floor. For a few seconds the buzz of computers being powered down challenged the creaking coming from the walls. People were picking up their bags and briefcases – Michael included, although he decided to leave his heavy laptop. After all, there was no reason to believe they would not be back in the office a little later on, and the laptop would be sitting there waiting for him. He called his wife Karen to tell her they had been ordered to leave the building but were not sure why, and he would be in touch once he reached the ground floor. Roselle, now Michael's close and constant shadow, was unfazed by the semi-panic around her. She saw Michael pick up his briefcase and that was enough to tell her they were going to be leaving the office early today.

'My friend, the Tower is tilting badly. It feels like it's going to fall into the street!' David yelled out as the screech of stretching metal grew louder and louder. The building was working hard to follow its in-built safety system and was fighting to correct itself. Like a prize fighter recovering from an enormous blow to his gut, the Tower was now pulling back and pushing up to its vertical position.

'Heel!' Michael called to Roselle, just to make sure she was with him. She responded immediately and was at his side in a second. Then, without warning, the floor dropped six feet as the building's expansion joints battled to do their job. Michael heard voices turn to screams.

'Oh my God, we've got to get out of here,' said David, reaching for Michael, who already had Roselle in harness. 'I'm looking out of the window and there's fire and office papers burning as they drift in the air. What the hell is going on? We need to get out of here. Let's go, my friend. Now!'

American Airlines flight 11 from Boston's Logan International Airport hit the north facade of the

North Tower at over 400 miles an hour, slicing through the building just fifteen floors above where Roselle was now leading Michael to the stairwell. David's instinct was to take the elevator, but something was telling Michael and urging Roselle to take the stairs. As the lights flickered overhead they felt the overpowering warmth in the walls and breathed in the hot stench that was creeping around them. The smell was odd but at the same time familiar. Michael knew he had smelled it before and searched his memory for the connection, looking for a clue to what was going on. Jet fuel. He recalled the smell from his many visits to airports all over the world, but why was there jet fuel in a skyscraper? What the hell?

There was no way Michael and his colleagues could see the ghostly carcass of the Boeing 767 airliner embedded in the opposite side of the building. For Michael and Roselle the journey through fear was about to begin in earnest.

Roselle was still calm. Her entire body was receptive to Michael's grip on her harness and, although she heard the screams and the raised and anxious voices echoing up and down the stairwell, her sense of calm transferred to her master. Two more floors down and the smell of kerosene was getting stronger. People were talking and reaching the conclusion that whatever was going on involved an aeroplane. Eight, ten floors down and the stairwell was getting crowded. 'Roselle … Hey, girl … You OK down

there? We'll be home soon. Don't you worry ...'
Michael attempted to comfort his dog and himself,
into the bargain.

Despite the heave of people now using the stairs
to get down and out to safety, Roselle remained calm
and took this in her stride. As the panic and uncer-
tainty rose and fell in the voices around them,
Michael heard people talking to Roselle. He knew
they would be stroking her and feeling for the
comfort of her warm coat and her breath on their
hands. He could feel fear, too, but right now Roselle's
safety was his focus.

Suddenly a woman appeared out of the swell of
grey smoke that was beginning to linger and fill their
space. 'Burns victim coming through! Burns victim
coming through!' The call made everyone push
aside for the group carrying their injured colleague.
The woman was very badly burnt. The skin on her
upper body had virtually melted away from the
bones. Michael felt the panic rise in the people
around him. The sight of this woman stopped his
colleagues in their tracks, and their gasps and tears
did nothing to ease Michael's growing anxiety.

Dropping on the stairs, a woman gave in to her
fear. 'I can't go on. I can't breathe,' she said as the
burns victim was carried past her. 'Oh my God, my
God, I can't do this.' In seconds the woman was
surrounded by her colleagues, all encouraging her to
get up and let them help her out of the building.

'We were suddenly faced with clear evidence that something very bad had happened and until then our confusion had sheltered us from it,' recalled Michael. 'What happened next was pure Roselle. I did not prompt her to do anything. She just sensed she was needed in a way that wasn't anything to do with being a guide dog.' Hearing the distress, Roselle stepped forward into the frightened woman's path. In an instant the woman had her arms around the dog's neck and Roselle's thick golden coat was soaking up the tears of fear that the woman could no longer hold back. The group took a moment to hug each other and at the centre of it all sat Roselle. The feeling of panic was now firmly in place, and as if being chased by a monster that was rapidly gaining ground on them, the group resumed their descent.

Thanks to Roselle's secret, silent canine brand of comfort, the group found themselves bonded in crisis and in their fight for survival. Giving himself the job of forward scout, David moved ahead of the group, taking a floor at a time and reporting back. Just as he became their voice in the dark, Roselle became their constant comforter.

9.15 a.m., Floor 30: 'Hop up, Roselle,' said Michael, encouraging his dog to pick up the pace, but he should have known that she instinctively knew the right pace on the stairs. Deferring to her skill and judgement, Michael allowed his guide dog to take the lead. 'I could sense that we still had some lights on the stairs, but then I realised that if they failed then we would all be blind. I wanted to lighten the atmosphere and say, "I'm a blind man and today we're offering a half-price special to get you out of here!" I was even thinking that when we got out of here we could arrange a reunion on the 78th floor at 8.45 a.m. the following morning and we could all celebrate. It was a bizarre thought, but nothing could be more bizarre than the situation we were in. We were running from an unknown enemy. Running as if our lives depended on it, and very soon we realised that they did.'

Final Expression of Unconditional Love

Roselle and Michael led the way, and as they rounded a crook in the stairs a shape in yellow and black loomed out of the grey. Fire fighters met them head-on. 'You OK, sir?' one asked, breathing heavily from the climb and the burden of the equipment he was carrying, which must have weighed at least 100 pounds. 'I'll escort you down the rest of the way.' Michael knew he didn't need the help. He knew that as long as he had Roselle at his side he would be fine. 'I told the guys there were people around me that were far more in need of help,' said Michael. 'I see blindness as a nuisance to me, not a disability, and a guide dog is not a given sign of vulnerability. For me, right there and then, Roselle was my strength, and more than that she was becoming a growing strength to others too. I wanted these brave guys to keep going and help those who really needed it. I know they didn't believe me, but I was fine. I had faith in my dog. Perhaps more faith than I had ever had in anything before in my life.'

The 9/11 Dogs

All this happened in seconds. There was no time to stand and debate. If a blind man didn't need help it was time to move on. 'I remember one of the fire fighters stopped for a moment and he looked into Roselle's eyes, knelt down and touched her face. She licked his hand. The deal was done. The fire fighter left us knowing that Roselle would take care of me. I was not alone. The moment when the uniformed giant passed me on his way up the stairs has haunted me ever since. Later, when the scale of the event became clear, I could not help thinking that Roselle's friendly lick could have been the last expression of unconditional love that man would feel in his life.'

The lobby was like a lake. There was water everywhere at the bottom of the stairs, where it was running in torrents from the sprinklers. It flowed down the escalators, forming pools where abandoned shoes floated around; their owners had long since passed by. Roselle stepped, belly deep, into the water to celebrate being free of the stifling heat and the close confines of the stairwell, before tagging onto the others being ushered out of the lobby space. Roselle wanted to get Michael outside, but she had to resist a natural urge to pull – her training would not allow her to do that, even though she was desperate to feel fresh air on her face.

Her training constantly battling her instincts, Roselle guided Michael through to the World Trade

Center shopping mall. Beyond that lay the outside world. It was hard on David, who could see the scene of dread confusion ahead: people running, others standing and staring up at the sky, fire rigs and other emergency-service vehicles scattered all over, and men on mobiles and hand-held radios directing people in the street.

9.40 a.m.: They had made it out and away from the North Tower, but David's sighted view of the world revealed a new fear. He looked around. 'My God, Michael,' he said. 'The South Tower is on fire.'

Michael looked down to speak to Roselle: 'OK … I'm in your hands now, girl. Get me out of here.'

Roselle, Michael and David hurried away, at first with David still half looking at the scene of devastation. On the west side of Broadway, Michael wanted to stop and call Karen. He'd promised her he would call her as soon as he knew more, and he needed to let her know that he was out of the Tower. Every call he made failed. The networks were jammed with the sheer volume of calls. It wasn't until later that everyone realised the calls were being made by those still trapped in the buildings. The calls for help, calls to say 'I love you', 'I'm sorry' and 'forgive me', and calls to say a final 'goodbye' streamed through the networks. As Michael struggled with the frustration of not being able to

reach his wife, Roselle trotted alongside him, eager
to get her master clear of the dangers. The air was
thick with the smell of jet fuel, and acrid smoke was
choking everyone in its path.

The South Tower stood a mere 100 yards away
from where Michael, Roselle and David were heading away a block at a time. Fingers of fire reached
down the Tower's glass flanks as waves of office
papers drifted from the gaping hole in its side and
down through the smoke to the streets below. David
couldn't help halting to take in the gruesomely
mesmerising scene around them, but he quickly
picked up on Roselle's need to keep moving. She had
led the way for the past hour and was showing no
sign of stopping. 'You know, looking back, I can see
that Roselle had one aim in her life from the moment
she left the North Tower,' recalls Michael. 'She was
going to get me home.'

Roselle sped along the sidewalks with Michael at
her side. Once David had caught up with them again
he quickly described what was going on around
them. There was danger in every direction, so
Michael chose his path – to carry on following
Roselle's lead. 'Roselle, we have to keep going. I'm
sure God would not want to save us from one building only to have us killed by another one falling on
us. We can do this, girl. I know you can do this with
me. David, what's that noise? Surely it wasn't a
thunderstorm?'

The distant rumble was not a thunderstorm. It was the shifting of the South Tower. Roselle had picked up the sound several seconds before anyone around her had felt the ground shake. 'Go right, go right!' David yelled, trying to protect them from behind and be heard above the tremendous roar that was growing louder and louder. Closer and closer. Roselle knew which way to go. She didn't need anyone to tell her, and Michael knew to follow her without question. Within minutes the deafening roar turned to a moment's silence before the crashing descent of the Tower sent a thick cloud of choking dust into the air.

Whatever they were running from, Michael guessed that it had caught up with them as Roselle veered off the street – and then suddenly stopped, stock still. To the blind man it felt as if they had stepped into a pit of human chaos, but no matter how much he tried to urge her on, Roselle refused to budge an inch. 'Please, help me!' a woman called out. 'I'm blind and afraid. There's dust in my eyes.' She was lying on the ground, her arms thrown over Roselle. A passer-by took Michael's arm and explained that his dog had stopped at the top of a steep flight of steps leading down to the subway. One more step and the woman, Michael and Roselle would have fallen. 'I realised that my guide dog had not only saved my life but saved another's too. I had to wonder', said Michael, 'if this dog was not just sent to lead me but to watch over me too. If not, then we both had a guardian angel.'

9.59 a.m.: The South Tower collapsed just fifty-six minutes after United Airlines flight 175 crashed into its southern face. The building that had formed part of the tallest man-made structure in the world when it was constructed was now a pile of rubble, shattered glass and melting metal. Covered in grey ash and splinters of debris, Roselle sat with Michael in the relative safety of the subway. Just a block away another guide dog, Salty, was leading his master, Omar Rivera, through the streets of Manhattan towards home.

Salty, My Friend and My Hero

8.15 a.m.: Salty's day had begun earlier than normal too. Omar Rivera worked for the Port Authority of New York and New Jersey, based in offices on the 71st floor of the North Tower. On a normal morning Omar and his guide dog would not have arrived much before 9 a.m., but on this particular day Omar was able to get a lift with a colleague, and Salty was quite happy to be there early to enjoy all the usual attention from the women in the office. Then he heard it – the voice he loved second best to his master's. It was Donna. Whenever Salty heard this voice he knew that he was in for a treat. 'Hi, Salty, you're in early today. Couldn't you sleep? What a good boy. Here's your breakfast treat. Don't tell Omar – I don't have a treat for him! See you later.'

Sitting at his desk with Salty settled underneath it in his basket, Omar was able to make a start on his work. The quiet in the office was just what he needed, but moments later all hell broke loose.

The 9/11 Dogs

'There was an incredible bang. The floor moved and sent me flying out of my chair, and as my hands lifted from my desk I heard my computer crash to the floor. The voices in the office grew louder and there was screaming all around me, and although I could hear the noise I could not hear what they were saying. And strangely, out of the deafening sound, I could still hear a flutter of papers and office furniture crashing around.'

Salty was first on his feet. Omar reached down – although he could sense that Salty was there, he needed to feel his guide dog's soft, warm coat in his hands, just to be sure. Putting out his hand he found the spiky hair on top of the big yellow Labrador's head and, reaching down further, he sunk both hands into the dog's thick fur and received a much-needed 'kiss' from his patient friend. 'Just knowing he was there meant my dark world was intact – for now, at least – and I took a moment to steady myself. I felt the intense heat on my skin and breathed in the strong smell of aviation fuel. I said my prayers and knew we had to get out, but Salty was already urging me to start walking.'

Salty was leading Omar towards the stairs where his colleagues were already crowding to get through the door and down to ground level. Omar could feel the heave of people around him, then, out of the push and shove, he felt a hand on his arm. It was his friend Donna, who had been frantic to find them.

'Thank God I've found you, Omar. I was so worried about you both. I will stay with you now.'

Salty reached the stairs. The space was crowded with screaming people choking on smoke. Underfoot, shards of glass and lumps of debris made each step into the gloom a painful leap of faith. 'Salty, are you OK?' Omar was worried about the glass that must have been digging into the dog's paws, and he wanted someone to check if Salty's eyes were streaming from the sting of the kerosene fumes circulating in the stairwell. Even if Salty was suffering any of these effects, he didn't complain – or about the water from the sprinklers, which was sloshing around his feet.

The water was a relief from the heat radiating from the walls, which crackled as they held back the blazing plane and its fuel, now pouring through the building. Omar remembered how, for a split second, the idea of making it out of the Tower alive in this chaos seemed impossible. 'People passed me on the stairs saying their prayers, asking God to keep them safe. I wondered if I was doing the best for Salty. I decided that if we were going to die here in this dark place then I needed to let him go free. I could not let my faithful companion down by making him stay with me and risk his own life. I whispered to him: 'Salty, you should leave me now. It's too dangerous for you to be here. Go now and I will see you when we both reach the bottom of the stairs. Go, my friend, before it's too late.'

The 9/11 Dogs

Salty understood the order. He stood still long enough to allow Omar to release the grip on his harness, but he would not leave his master's side. 'Go, Salty. Leave me now,' said Omar, pushing his dog forwards. His colleagues tried to help, but the sad sight of the dog, who clearly did not want to go anywhere without his master, was too much to bear. They tried to encourage the dog to run ahead, but he would not go. Clearly, wherever Omar was going, Salty would be at his side. As he replaced his guide dog's harness, Omar knew he had to accept that Salty would be with him to the end.

Comfort for the Dying

9.30a.m.: With thirty floors still to negotiate before they reached ground level, Salty's reluctance to leave Omar's side became an inspiration to Donna and the other hopefuls on the stairs. Omar cuddled his dog in his arms: 'I stroked Salty and told him how happy I was that he was my dog. I felt Donna kneel down and spread her arms around him and I imagined his big golden head resting on her shoulder. He was always my hero, but now he was everyone's hero, and I felt honoured to know this beautiful dog. I told him: "Salty, your calmness and reassurance is every-thing we need to help us the rest of the way. I know you will be the reason why we have every chance of survival."'

With Salty leading the group, ahead of Omar and Donna, there was calmness in the ranks. But three flights down a bottleneck of people was beginning to form as fire fighters carrying emergency packs and breathing equipment were heading up to check for survivors on higher floors. Those who were determined to get out of the Tower quickly met the dying and the injured waiting for assistance on the stairs.

Salty made his way to the worst of the casualties and wandered between them, meeting their outstretched hands. Touching his head and body, the people smiled, spoke to him and reached for him, gaining some comfort before he moved on, making a pathway for Omar and guiding him safely through. The dim, intermittent lighting was not a problem for Salty or Omar, but others found it difficult to focus and negotiate the stairs. Letting Salty lead the way speeded up the descent, and within an hour and fifteen minutes Omar and his colleagues had made it down from the 71st floor, only to find the lobby awash with water from the sprinklers and littered with survivors unsure of where to go next. Fire fighters directed Omar and the rest of his group towards the street, where the confusion spread.

Hitting the street, Salty was back on familiar territory. With Omar safely at his side, Salty set a pace to get them to safety. The snowstorm of debris from the fall of the South Tower persisted between the buildings, enveloping the scene indiscriminately, spitting grey ash. Running along the sidewalks they met people scarred by the fire and the falling debris that had caught in their clothes and hair. Aviation fuel that had escaped from the planes as they crashed into the Twin Towers had dripped onto everything in its path, or raced in sheets of flame, causing

horrific injuries to anyone it met. Some people were
running, but others were too dazed to run anywhere.

Even twenty blocks away from Ground Zero, the
dust crept over and into everything. The fallout
from the collapse of the South Tower almost
submerged man and dog. Like two ghostly appari-
tions, they ran on in search of safety and a pathway
home.

Chaos in the Ruins

10.28 a.m.: After burning for 102 minutes, the North Tower finally collapsed. The structure – almost sliced in two by the hijacked airliner – could take no more and fell to the ground. Roselle and Michael were taking shelter in the subway when the news reached them. The sudden arrival of more people piling into the station prompted Michael to ask someone what was going on. 'The North Tower is down and there's only a ball of fire and smoke where the World Trade Center once stood,' was a stranger's description of what the man and his dog had just escaped.

Roselle was still comforting the woman blinded by the dust from the collapse of the South Tower. She was cradling the Labrador like a baby and holding her so tight it was as if she was afraid of what would happen if she let go. More people started to appear in the subway. With them a medical unit immediately honed in on the woman clinging to Roselle. As the woman was now in safe hands,

Michael decided it was time to move on and prompted Roselle to venture out onto the street. Somehow she found her bearings, despite the distractions and confusion they met as soon as they emerged into the grey world above.

Michael wanted to head to the house of a friend on the edge of the city, but did Roselle understand this in the confusion? She had been there before and was somehow reminded that she could make it there again. Without stopping to think or question Roselle's actions, Michael held onto his dog and let her take him – man and dog were thinking and moving as one. After all, she had a view on the world that Michael could only imagine, and the choking dust was enough for him to battle against as they ran on and on through the wall of sirens and screams.

As if in a bubble that contained just a man and his dog, Michael trusted wherever Roselle led. The world he could hear but not see was in chaos, and all he could do was seek sanctuary. Block after block they ran, until eventually they emerged from the wreckage, shocked and mired in dust, and walked into the welcoming arms of their friends. How Roselle had found them seemed, in everyone's eyes, to be a miracle.

Not far away from the house where Roselle was then resting from her ordeal, Salty arrived on the doorstep of his family's home in New Jersey. As the Rivera family opened the door they almost didn't recognise the grey figures that stood in front of them. Running for their lives, Salty and Omar had made it home, and it seemed to everyone that this, too, was a miracle. With eyes full of tears of relief and arms outstretched, Omar told his family: 'I owe my life to Salty, my companion and my best friend.'

The Search for Life

By 10.30 a.m. the Twin Towers were a just a fallen pile of concrete and tortured metal. The phone lines to the Towers had been jammed for over an hour, and the city's 911 system had been overwhelmed with calls. Patrol cars and fire rigs were stationed at every turn on every block, within and outside the impact zone, and their sirens created a constant wall of sound. Carnage erupted as the terror in the World Trade Center spilled out onto the streets. People slumped onto the sidewalk in a state of shock, many nursing horrific injuries: a woman sat holding her head in her heavily blood-stained hands; another staggered to a halt, the back of her jacket melted to her skin. Hands, faces and limbs were snagged and scored with shards of shattered glass.

The evacuation of Lower Manhattan began in earnest shortly after the fall of the South Tower. Attention focused on the people still trapped inside its sister building. Many of the workers on the opposite side of the North Tower had no view of what was going on. One man had called his wife from the 86th floor to tell her that he loved her and that he had no idea what was going on, but he knew he had to get out. He tried the door to stairwell C but it was twisted, so he struck the dry wall with a crowbar and broke through. He joined others jostling their way down the dimly lit stairs, and within seconds of hitting the street they were running for their lives.

'Get away from the Tower! Get away from the Tower!' The calls came loud and repeated as the building's 1,000-foot-long crumbling shadow chased them down. Lost inside the ruins were hundreds of office staff and the emergency workers who had fearlessly swept each floor up to the point of impact for survivors. The slump of the second Tower was followed by an eerie hush, broken only by the music still playing from the underground shopping mall.

A pall of thick grey ash lingered over the pile, mingling with the smoke rising from the crushed masonry and steel framework, and scattered over the burning heaps of debris. Fire fighters tore at the rubble with their bare hands. When the call went out that morning, 14,000 fire fighters and paramedics were deployed to the Twin Towers: more than 2,000 of them became trapped in the impact zone. Voices called up from the ruins and rescuing hands reached down into the fire and ash. Frantically clawing at steel girders and concrete blocks, emergency workers fought on towards their stranded fellows entombed in what now resembled a sinister multi-layered cake of colours and textures. Everything that had been vertical was now horizontal and swarming with police and fire crews forming 'bucket brigades' to shift the dirt and debris as fast as possible.

1.28 p.m.: The first search dogs arrived at Ground Zero and got to work immediately. Dogs from the New York Police Department K-9 Unit and New York Fire Department eagerly hit the pile, not knowing in which direction to start.

One of the first dogs on the scene was Appollo, a veteran police search dog who was a little grey at the muzzle and had an eye on retirement, but whose experience on the ground was unrivalled. The German Shepherd's lean body would have given any younger dog a run for its money, and he would have walked into hell for his handler, police officer Pete Davies. When Pete received the call to duty that day it was like any other emergency, with strict procedures to follow before the team could carry out the order: 'Get to the World Trade Center site and get there quickly.'

Appollo was used to the drill and sat patiently while Pete strapped on his official reflective jacket and packed fresh water, food and essential equipment for man and dog, as he had done many times during his twenty years as a New York City police officer. 'The station had been handling running reports and requests from Ground Zero since the first plane hit at 8.46 a.m., but nothing could have prepared any member of the search-and-rescue team for the scale of the devastation that met us when we arrived on the scene,' recalled Pete. 'I had attended countless rescue situations with Appollo over our eight years as a partnership, but my first sight of Ground Zero was one of despair. Thinking back, I guess it was clear to many of the teams that the search for life would be very short.'

Appollo was his usual eager self, literally straining at his leash to get to work. Sniffing the dirty air, he sneezed repeatedly, and Pete could see that the thick dust and ash mix was going to be a problem for his dog's eyes too. Already its sticky greyness was collecting on his heavy black coat, and his ginger-brown underbelly was losing its sheen. It would usually take hours for normal masonry dust to collect like this, but this was not normal and the effect was almost immediate.

Pete had plenty of water in his bag and he knew he would need every drop. The initial team of six dogs and handlers checked in with the Federal Emergency Management Agency (FEMA) officials and took their first steps onto the site, already named Ground Zero. Appollo was well up for the search, and as he swaggered towards his first view of the pile his eyes immediately focused on what lay directly ahead. He was shoulder to shoulder with danger but still trotted ahead of Pete, who was taking in his own view of the carnage.

Nose so near to the ground it was almost touching the cinders, Appollo switched into search mode. For the first few seconds of the search Pete was the partnership's eyes and ears, as Appollo concentrated everything on his sense of smell. Taken by a moment of sheer disbelief at the magnitude of the task in hand, Pete turned briefly away from his dog, who was working less than six feet ahead. In that split second Pete turned back to see Appollo disappear headfirst into the pile.

Striding forward without thought or caution, Pete reached into the fiery pit and pulled Appollo from the embers, patting the flames that immediately caught his smouldering coat. 'I saw Appollo ahead of me and knew he would just get on with his job. To be honest, I really couldn't believe the enormity of the devastation all around me. It was just too much to take in and make what would normally be a logical decision, so I decided to let Appollo make his own way over the pile and I would follow, picking up signs and sounds along the way. He knew what to do, and if there was life to be found there I knew Appollo would locate it.

'But when I saw the last flick of his tail disappear into the ash, something powerful came over me. I'm not sure how I got to him and I'm not sure how I caught him as he was falling, but it happened, and once I had him in my arms there was no way I could let go until I knew that he was OK. This dog saved my life so many times during his career. This was already our toughest test imaginable.' Taking hold of Appollo, Pete rushed him away to check him over and allow him to rest for a while. Within an hour Appollo was back searching the pile, with only a patch of singed fur on his belly to show for his ordeal.

If there was life to be found in the chaos and the wreckage, time was rapidly running out.

'Duty. Honour. Country'

Dotted about between the ruins, the search-and-rescue dogs made their presence felt. The sight of the determined German Shepherds, Labradors and Retrievers gave hope to the uniformed officers digging frantically to find their buddies. Very soon, shouts for 'Dog over here!' could be heard all over the pile as the whine of fire fighters' electric locators rose out of the rubble. As each one tripped, a fellow officer ran to tap on the wreckage in the hope of a response from below.

Fires that were probably ignited by the jet fuel were being sustained by the vast amount of paper and wood from the thousands of square metres of office space. The almost lunar landscape of ash was a shifting surface that made the search difficult and dangerous for dog and handler. But the world that lay under the columns of twisted steel and concrete was one that could only be accessed through a canine's hyper-sensitive sense of smell. Trained to detect traces of blood, flesh, sweat and other odours

42

emitted by the human body in times of stress, the dogs were to be the key to rescuing life and, sadly, recovering remains. If the dogs couldn't find anything in this chaos, no human stood a chance.

New York police officer Suzanne McCrossan was supposed to be on leave that day, but she didn't need a call from her chief to make her realise that all leave was cancelled. Quickly changing into her uniform and grabbing her faithful search dog, Charlie, she made for her police vehicle and headed for the city precinct. Golden Retriever Charlie knew they were going to work, so he was excited and typically eager to get into his distinctive NYPD K-9 jacket.

Only two weeks back from maternity leave, Suzanne left her husband and baby daughter knowing this deployment would be unlike any other. She recalled: 'The news reports were more like scenes from a movie than real life in downtown Manhattan. I recognised the buildings, but everything else was unreal, and as I left my family, with Charlie at my side, I only knew one thing for sure and that was that Charlie would look after me, as he always did. I trusted him to keep me safe.'

Suzanne made it as far as the outskirts of the impact zone before she hit the full horror of the job in hand. She reached down to pat Charlie, still innocently wagging his tail in anticipation of a 'find'. Gathering all her equipment and taking a firm grasp of Charlie's long lead, Suzanne left the dog van to start her walk in. Clouds of ash still lingered in the air, and all the time people coated in its greyness were passing her like ghosts, in silence or in tears. Their hollow expressions were something Suzanne will never forget: 'I wanted to ask people if they were OK and where they were going, but their expressions appeared to answer all the questions I could ever ask.'

Charlie looked at every person as they passed, and some could not help putting their hand down to him, which he met with his usual rub and lick. For some, this was too much and they simply fell to their knees and wept as they hugged him. Charlie took the attention well, but Suzanne was aware that they had to get to Ground Zero as quickly as possible. She quietly explained to people why they needed to break away and that others were relying on Charlie to be there to rescue them and help them to safety. 'I felt sad doing this, but I did not want to let my colleagues down. After all, these people were safe and many others were not.'

Arriving on site, Suzanne made herself known to the Federal Emergency Management Agency (FEMA) team and prepared to go onto the pile. She had not yet taken a step onto the still-hot ground when Charlie was spotted by a group of fire fighters working their way through the debris covering the skeleton of a rig. Its burnt-out chassis mangled almost beyond recognition, the vehicle, she could just make out, was the likely resting place of several of her comrades. 'Dog over here! Please send your dog over here,' they called. Suzanne let Charlie bound ahead of her and he was met with several outstretched hands. In any other situation, this would have been unusual, as the men knew better than to touch the dog while he was working. But the reaction was instant and natural and could not be helped.

They said they had heard knocking from under the wreckage, which was almost entirely covered by a column of concrete. Charlie did not need an invitation to start work. Within five minutes the dog had begun to dig towards the rear of the rig, which had been used as a water hose on the site, and the call went out to investigate the 'find'. The second call was for one of the orange body bags, which was passed on down the line to where Charlie stood.

Moving further over and under the visible parts of the vehicle, his nose now powdered with dust, Charlie began padding on the ground. The men listened hard for noise from beneath the rubble for an indication of life from their colleagues. But the second call for a body bag removed all hope of that. With two bodies located and in such extreme condition, it was clear to the rest of the crew that hope was fading for the others. Suzanne noticed that Charlie was in need of water and that his eyes were clouding with the dust. She reached for a bottle of water, but before she could pull it free of her bag, one of the fire fighters had his canteen ready, and, pouring the water into a colleague's hand, they offered the dog a much-needed drink.

Charlie worked beyond the call of duty those first few hours he was on the pile. If there was any chance of finding life, it was then. FEMA was aware that the work of the search-and-rescue teams was going to be vital, particularly in the early phase of the operation, and issuing a nationwide call for dog teams to come forward resulted in a massive response from all over the United States of America.

Police task forces from as far away as California answered the call, and those living locally began the trek into the city. For two Vietnam veterans and their dogs, Tsunami and Cody Bear, the journey in from Long Island was made without question. When asked why he volunteered for the search at Ground Zero, Major Paul Morgan, a retired US Marine, replied: 'Duty. Honour. Country.'

Healing for the Heroes

On Tuesday 11 September, the Suffolk County Society for the Prevention of Cruelty to Animals (SPCA) received a call from the New York City K-9 units assigned to rescue at the World Trade Center. It was a desperate call for the Suffolk County SPCA MASH unit to report to Ground Zero immediately to provide veterinary care to the brave and exhausted rescue dogs working on the pile.

By 6 p.m. the unit was set up on West Street, two blocks away from Ground Zero and in the heart of the aftermath. Six law-enforcement agents had escorted the MASH unit through the chaos to ensure its safe passage and so that the staff could set up as soon as possible. As the fully equipped mobile treatment centre arrived on site, it entered a different world. The acrid smoke, loud sirens and cries of panic and fear created one of the most chaotic scenes any member of the team had ever witnessed. There was no doubt that they needed to get to work.

Calls went out to Long Island veterinarians. The New York Veterinary Hospital and the Animal Medical Center returned the call, and right away veterinarians and vet technicians were placed on twelve-hour schedules, starting at 6 p.m. Using police radio bands, the New York City Office of Emergency Management (OEM) was advised of the unit's location and purpose – to provide immediate medical care to all rescue dogs and pets in the vicinity. A self-contained hospital with an operating theatre, the MASH unit was equipped to handle all veterinary emergencies. But this was far beyond a state of emergency.

That evening, dog rescue teams from the metropolitan area were the first on the scene. The dogs had worked continuously with only breaks for water since arriving at Ground Zero, and they only left the pile when the handlers and the dogs were on the verge of collapse.

Dehydration was the main enemy of the search dog, and the MASH unit was equipped with massive amounts of intravenous fluid. Even though more dogs were arriving to search, all the teams were set to work twenty-plus hours on the pile. It was a race against time and the dogs were their best hope.

By Thursday more help had arrived. Supplies came in and tents were put up to protect the veterinary staff from the rain. Four stations for washing and treating dogs were put in place. Four vets and four vet technicians were working full-time, examining and treating these courageous animals.

The first two days were brutal …

Brave Dogs Will Not Rest

John Charos had booked a day's leave for 9/11. He wasn't supposed to be anywhere near New York that day. But as fortune would have it, this veterinarian was home watching the news on television. When the call came in he was determined to offer help. Dr Charos added supplies to his veterinarian's bag, got into his car and drove towards the city. When he arrived the scene that met him looked, in his own words, 'like the end of the world'.

Abandoning his car on the edge of the impact zone, he began to walk towards Ground Zero and into the ash cloud that had fallen over Lower Manhattan. Everywhere he looked people sat dazed and confused by the scenes they had witnessed. There were people from apartments close to the World Trade Center wandering around clutching their pets for security and strength. Dr Charos checked the pets over as he passed through, and at the same time comforted the owners.

The MASH unit operation was underway, and already a number of the Ground Zero heroes were being checked over. The handlers were keen to make sure their dogs were OK, but at the same time eager to get back to work. By their terms, the longer they spent off the pile the less chance they had of locating a person alive. Dr Charos was straight away part of the nation's hope: 'The love of a dog for its skills in the service of humanity is one thing, but respect for a dog as a partner in the face of extreme adversity is something extraordinary. What I witnessed was love and devotion and determination in the bond between the handlers and their dogs. The feeling and emotion was so evident you could almost touch it.'

Day two dawned and the fires were still burning beneath Ground Zero. Volunteer canine search teams were joining the police and fire-service dogs who had been working a twelve- to fifteen-hour stretch. Injured, dehydrated and exhausted, they worked on. By day three the rescue teams were still hearing the electronic locators worn by the buried fire fighters bleeping from under the ruins.

By this time the veterinarians and tech staff at the MASH unit were not only dealing with fatigued animals; they were also seeing burns and blistered feet as a result of the heat on the pile. Protective boots were issued immediately, but not all the dogs could work in them, and for some they were an uncomfortable distraction. Another new problem was canine stress. For dogs trained to find life, this was a very depressing and frustrating time. Without life, there is no reward for these highly skilled and deeply instinctive dogs.

Day four – the city was being wallpapered with the images of people lost and missing, and the names of the dead were being declared. For the dogs, this was no longer a rescue operation.

Carrying a Nation's Hope

No one could ever have anticipated the massive amount of support that would be required for the logistical operation of the canine search teams to accomplish the mission at the World Trade Center. Suffolk County SPCA Incident Commander Gerry Lauber took the initial call from the NYPD K-9 unit requesting support for the search-and-rescue dogs at Ground Zero and offered an immediate response. 'No one could believe what they saw when we arrived at the site. Many described it as close to a war zone or world's end. One thing that was very clear was that there was no time to waste. The search-and-rescue dogs were on site and they needed our help. If they were going to find anyone alive then we needed to provide essential veterinary support.'

Within five days the Suffolk County SPCA had set up ten fully functioning work stations supported by a veterinarian and a vet technician, and for forty days the MASH unit provided on-site care not only for the dogs, but for the pets of those evacuated from the nearby apartments.

Chief of Department Roy Gross said: 'Local residents from local apartments who left their pets behind when the buildings were evacuated sought our help too. Security at the pile was extremely tight, which limited what we could physically achieve in terms of rescuing pets, but the circumstances were so extreme and the Suffolk County SPCA were the only humane agency allowed on the site, so we did what needed to be done.'

In addition to the active involvement with the treatment of the search-and-rescue dogs – providing over 700 treatments to more than 300 dogs – the staff of the MASH unit also rescued over thirty pets and gave them medical assistance. One cat was rescued after eighteen days of isolation in the debris.

And all the time, the dogs were on duty.

Canine Therapy

'I can't cry in front of my fellow officers, but I can cry in the presence of a dog. He won't judge me. He won't deride me or think me stupid. He will just look into my eyes and know what I'm thinking and feel what I'm feeling. This is the power of a dog's unconditional love.' A police officer desperate to find a colleague lost in the debris of Ground Zero slumps into exhaustion. He moves away from the site, just for a while, and joins a nearby fire crew sitting together in silence. Forced to retire from the scene for a short break, they see one of the rescue dogs approaching with his handler. The police officer drops to his knees and holds out his arms to the dog. As if he knows exactly what the man needs from him, the dog moves forward and licks the man's face. Enveloped in the man's arms, the dog dutifully sits and stays. He is there for as long as the man needs to cry and reach out for comfort.

Any dog lover will tell you that when you need unconditional love most of all, a dog will sense it and provide it without question. For the emergency services working at Ground Zero and the Pentagon, the dogs were not only a constant symbol of hope on site; they became a source of therapy too. For the hurt and the loss that could not be expressed in words to another human being, there were the dogs, always ready to absorb the emotion and blot out the trauma. As one fire fighter said: 'When you cry on a dog's shoulder he just absorbs the tears and says everything by saying nothing.'

Remembering the Loved and the Lost

As companion or protector, whether providing a skilled service or serving as a lovable mascot, a dog will always give more of itself than first meets the eye – more than any person could promise in courage, loyalty and love.

Dogs are the eternal levellers, the non-judgemental friend. They are capable of displaying a quality of character that distinguishes the extraordinary from the ordinary, providing comfort where there is pain, and calm where there is confusion.

But a dog really comes into its own when the chances of survival are against all the odds, and only the brave and the devoted and those prepared to go beyond the call of duty will stand as heroes among the many.

Whether dogs are aware of their courage or not does not really matter. On 11 September 2001 and during its aftermath they provided practical support in the field as a result of their training, and gave those involved spiritual support as well. To many, their warmth matched their truth and integrity. The courage of these special dogs is boundless.

On the morning of the canine bravery ceremony in March 2002, I saw three dogs step forward in the company of many others to receive the highest reward for their courage on 9/11. Guide dogs Salty and Roselle stepped up to have their medals placed around their necks. And veteran search dog Appollo accepted the large bronze medal on behalf of the entire team of more than 300 dogs and handlers who risked all during their time at Ground Zero.

Applause echoed through the cold and over the waterfront. Watching the ceremony were many of the veterinarians who had treated the dogs during their time on site, employees of the World Trade Center and Port Authority, and the friends and family of the men saved by their guide dogs. All these people were brought together in that place, on that morning, to honour their heroes – the dogs that saved them in so many ways.

As everyone left the presentation and made their way to Ground Zero to pay their respects, I noticed people reach for each other. Hands were held. Arms were placed on shoulders. Hugs were given as tears fell. For many, this was the first time they had been back to the site since that terrible day in September 2001. They were going back there to honour the dogs: the dogs who had saved their lives or inspired them to keep going. The dogs of Ground Zero would be their forever heroes.

On that September morning, New York stood still and nearly 3,000 human lives were lost. It was one of the most horrific events in global history – and dogs played their part in the face of human tragedy. The dogs went in to bring life out, and the authorities knew that, if it was there, the dogs would find it. For hours and days after the terrorist attack on the Twin Towers the search-and-rescue dogs carried a nation's hope on their backs and worked as if they knew it.

As one New York firefighter said:

'The dogs who saved their life rescued their soul from despair and inspired them not to give up or give in.'

These were the dogs of 9/11.

Moving Memoirs

Stories of hope, courage and the power of love…

If you loved this book, then you will love our
Moving Memoirs eNewsletter

Sign up to…

- Be the first to hear about new books

- Get sneak previews from your favourite authors

- Read exclusive interviews

- Be entered into our monthly prize draw to win one
  of our latest releases before it's even hit the shops!

Sign up at

www.moving-memoirs.com

Harper True.
Time to be inspired

Write for us

Do you have a true life story of your own?

Whether you think it will inspire us, move us, make us laugh or make us cry, we want to hear from you.

To find out more, visit

www.harpertrue.com or send your ideas to harpertrue@harpercollins.co.uk and soon you could be a published author.